Measure and Compare

by Clare O'Brien

Table of Contents

Y0-DJP-702

I need to know these words.

alligator

Eiffel Tower

pig

pony

roller coaster

Space Needle

How Can You Measure and Compare?

Do you like to ride roller coasters? You can ride high in the air! You can **measure** the heights of roller coasters.

▲ The Giant Dipper is 180 feet high.

One roller coaster is one hundred eighty feet high. The other roller coaster is seventy-three feet high. You can **compare** the numbers. The number one hundred eighty is **greater than** the number seventy-three.

▲ The Rattler is 73 feet high.

You can measure buildings, too. The Space Needle is six hundred thirty feet high. The Eiffel Tower is nine hundred eighty-four feet high.

▲ The Space Needle is in Seattle.

You can compare the **heights**. The Eiffel Tower is taller than the Space Needle.

▲ The Eiffel Tower is in Paris.

Which Number Is Smaller?

An alligator has a large mouth. Some alligators have eighty teeth! A horse has about thirty-six teeth. The number thirty-six is **less than** the number eighty.

▲ A horse has fewer teeth than an alligator.

Two boys count their teeth. Then the boys compare the numbers of teeth. Jack has twenty-four teeth. Ryan has twenty-six teeth. Who has fewer teeth?

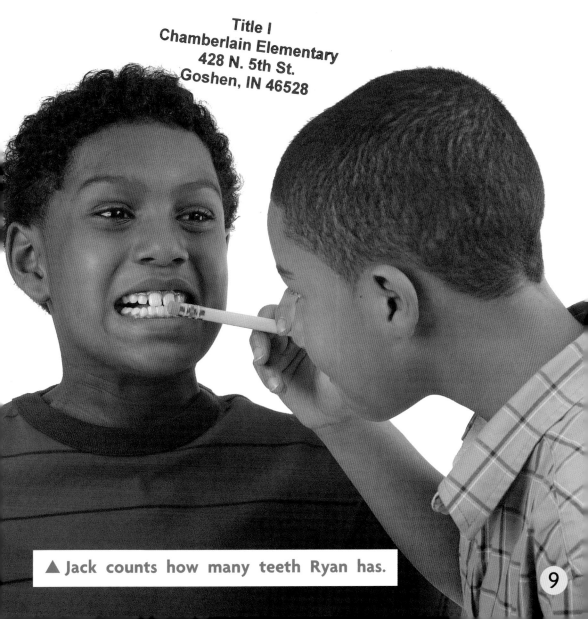

▲ Jack counts how many teeth Ryan has.

A pig is heavy. Some pigs are heavier than other pigs. You can compare these three pigs.

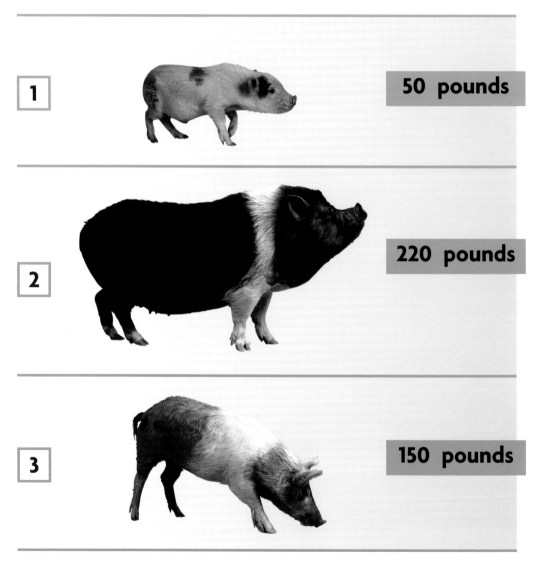

1   **50 pounds**

2   **220 pounds**

3   **150 pounds**

▲ **Which pig weighs the least?**

You can compare other animals, too. A pony is very heavy. Compare the pony to the goat.

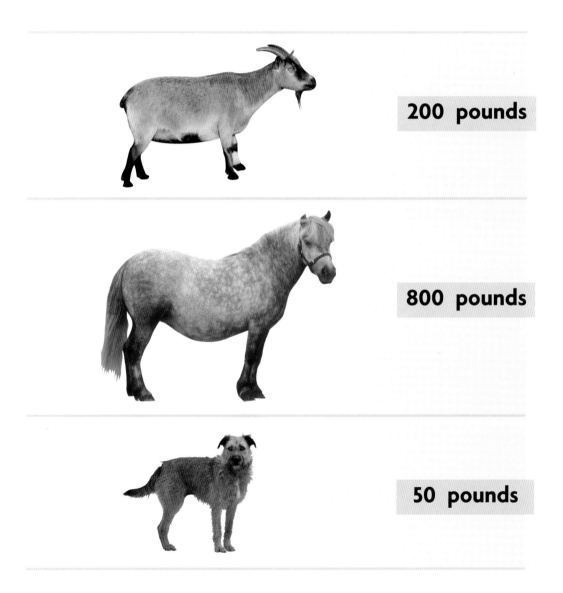

200 pounds

800 pounds

50 pounds

▲ How much less does the goat weigh?

Can Numbers Be Equal?

Molly lives in Dallas. Molly will go to Houston soon. The distance between the two cities is two hundred forty miles.

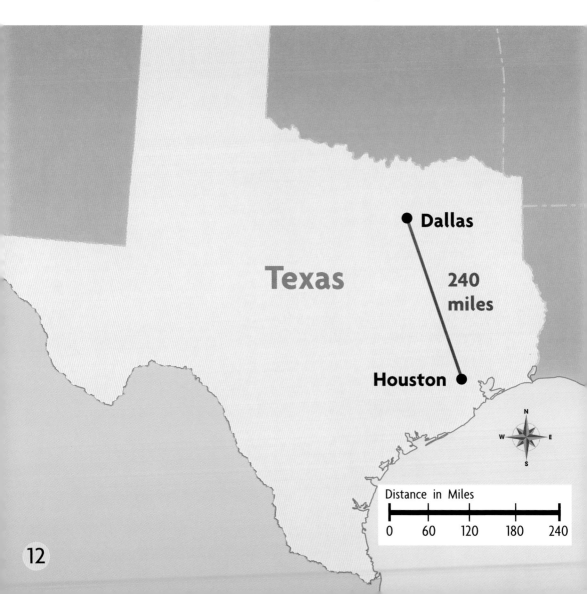

Dallas

Texas

240 miles

Houston

Distance in Miles

0   60   120   180   240

Sue lives in Memphis. Sue will travel to Birmingham. She will travel two hundred forty miles. Molly and Sue will travel the same distance. The distances are **equal**.

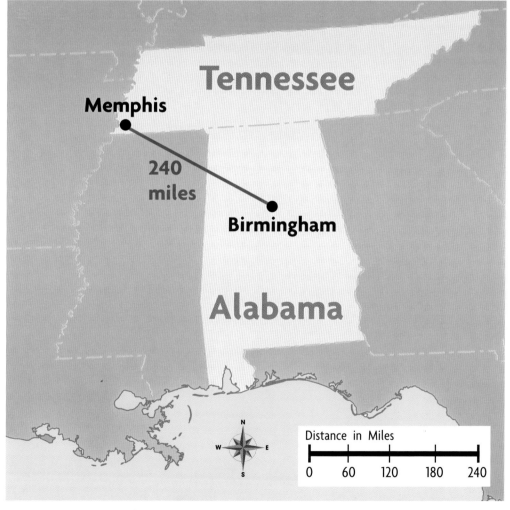

▲ Two hundred forty miles is equal to 240 miles.

Dave lives in New York. Dave will visit Jack. Jack lives in Baltimore. Baltimore is about two hundred miles away.

Dave will visit Meg. Meg lives in Boston. Boston is about two hundred miles from New York. The distances are the same.

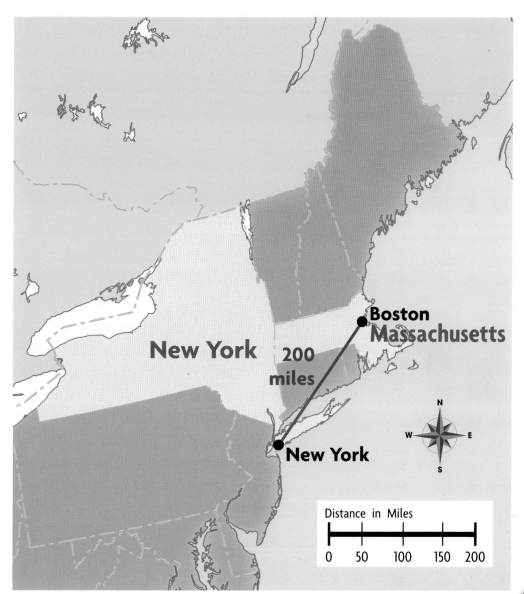

Which Number Is Greater?

Look at these dogs. Some dogs are tall. Some dogs are short. Which dog is the shortest?

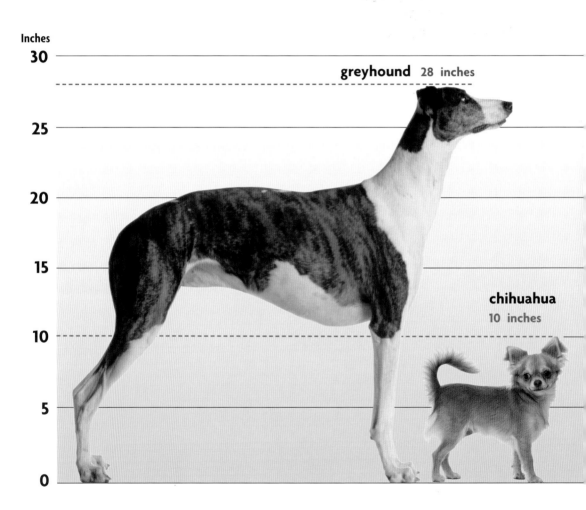

Inches

greyhound 28 inches

chihuahua 10 inches

Look at the chart. You can compare the heights of the dogs. Which dog is the tallest? Put the dogs in order by height.

Inches

30

collie
25 inches

25

20

beagle
17 inches

15

10

5

0

▲ The beagle is 17 inches tall. Which dogs are taller than the beagle?

17

Three children want to compare heights. Look at the children. Look at the numbers. You can compare the heights of the children.

Centimeters

145 centimeters

125 centimeters

110 centimeters

150

120

90

60

30

0

Amy   Charlie   Maria

▲ Charlie is taller than Amy. Maria is taller than Charlie.

Numbers tell you many things. Look at the chart. Which numbers are bigger? Which numbers are smaller?

Measurement	Girl	Giraffe
height	4 feet	16 feet
weight	75 pounds	1,500 pounds
length of neck	3 inches	96 inches

Glossary

compare (kum-PAIR): to find out how things are alike or different See page 5.

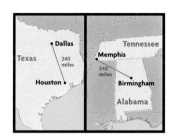

equal (EE-kwul): the same in amount, size, number, or value See page 13.

greater than (GRATE-er THAN): larger in number See page 5.

height (HITE): how high something is See page 7.

less than (LES THAN): smaller in number See page 8.

measure (MEH-zher): to find the size or amount of; to find out how long, wide, or large something is See page 4.

Index